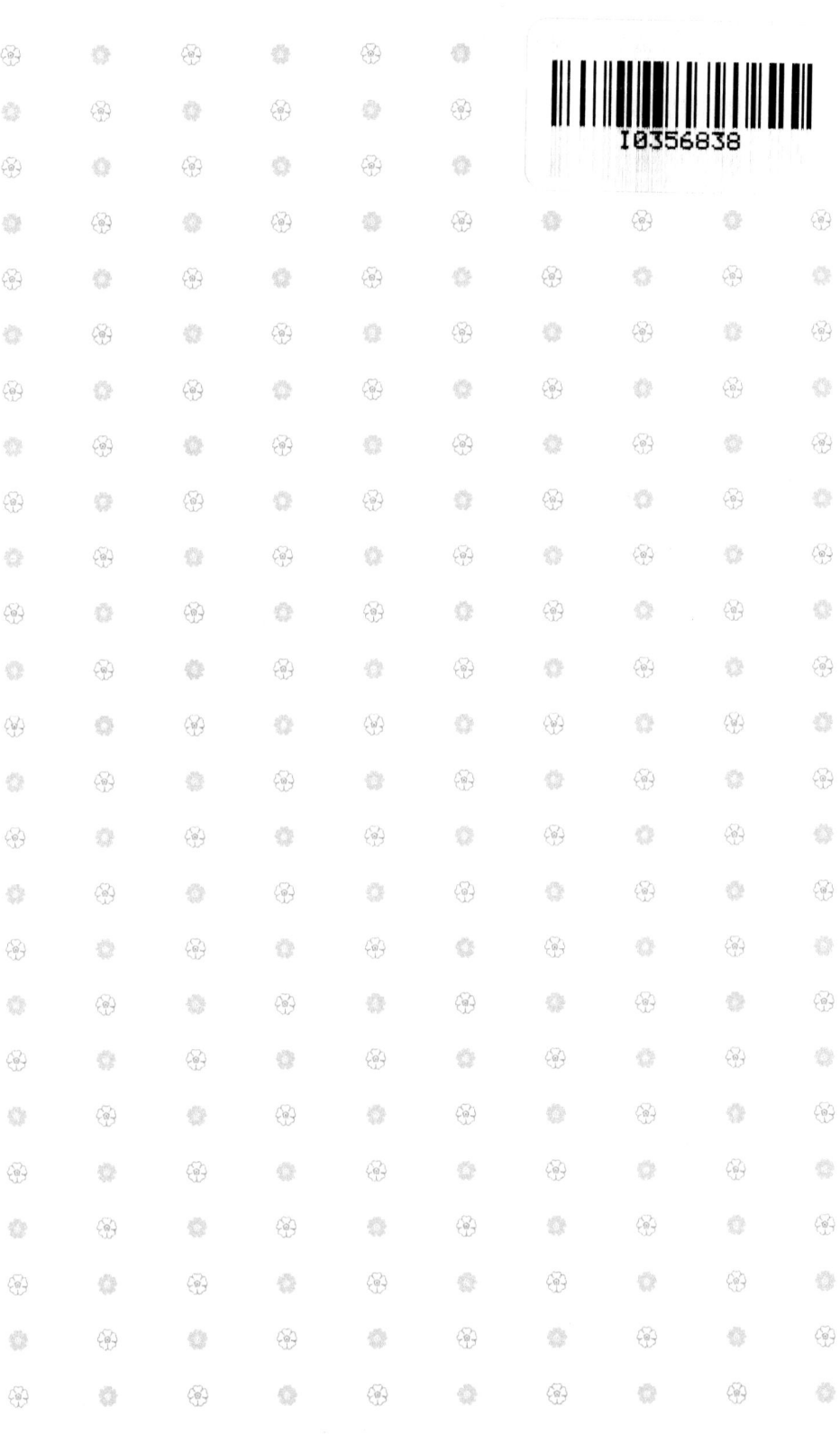

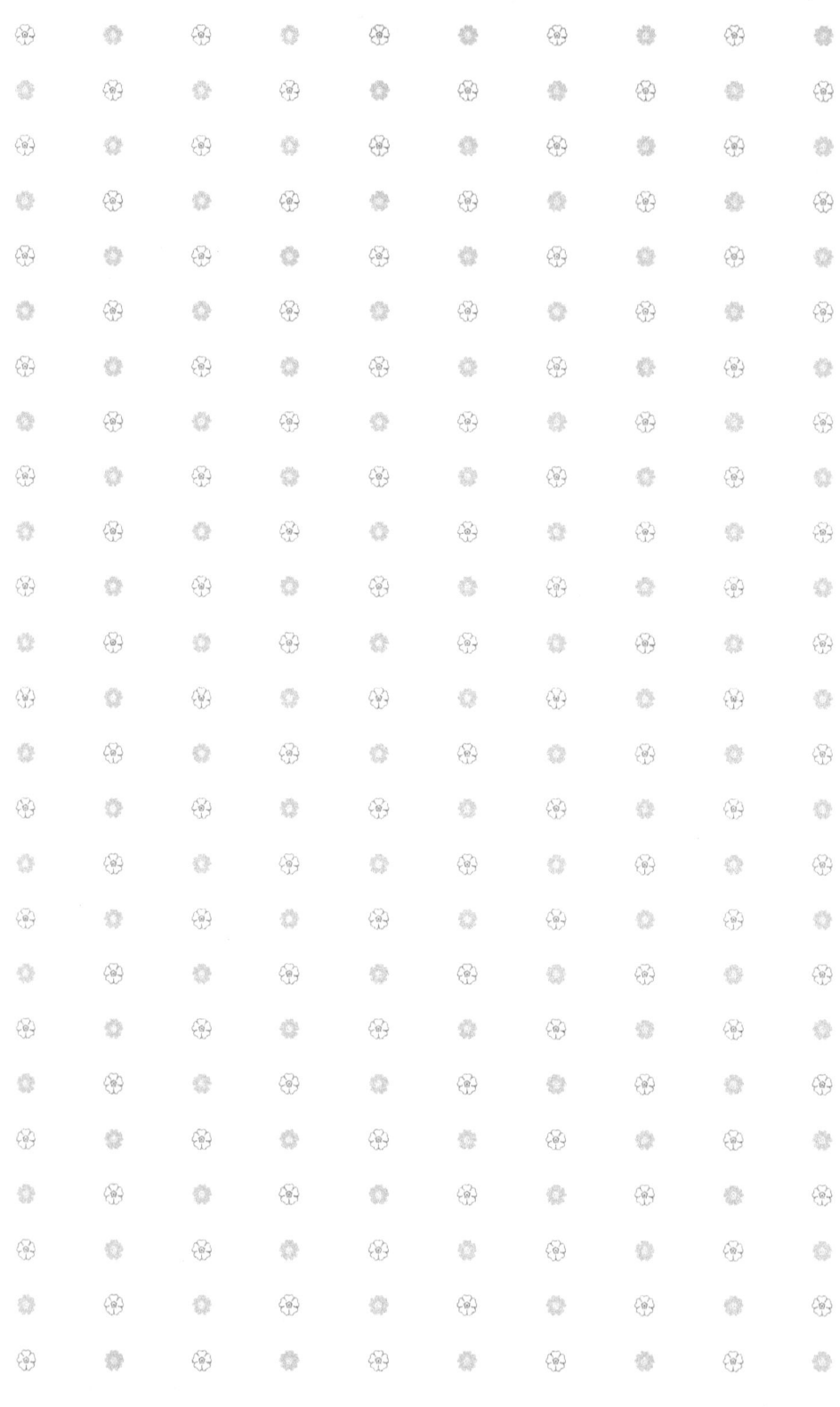

in case of emergency press

We are proud to acknowledge the Traditional Owners of country throughout Australia and to recognise their continuing connection to land, waters, and culture. We pay our respects to their Elders.

We support recognition, reconciliation, and reparation.

Praise for Point Blank

What is it to be *seen*? To never know, at any moment, if you're the viewer or the viewed? In this world where an ID "pries the past" from you, and your present is left composed of the "thousand tiny data points that track/what's left of who you are", poet Gary Duehr reminds us what it is to truly *see* and reconstitutes our humanity from a cyber-driven economy that sees us as "a thing to buy and use". Duehr's poems deftly span the decades and their technologies, from the sixties with its enchantment with Technicolor ("in color everyone is walking towards the future") to the present with its small screen in the palm of every hand, where every bad decision published there makes "you wish you could reverse/the flow of time". At one point in his masterful meditations, Duehr asks "Who among us will bear witness?" These poems step up to do their part, reminding us what it is to be fully human in these most difficult of times.

Catherine Sasanov,
author of *Had Slaves*

Poet Gary Duehr—also a photographer of the unnoticed, the ordinary made newly strange—brings his insatiable camera-eye to these poems. Here are the mysteries of strangers in transitional spaces—airports, street corners—identities and purposes unknown and wildly potent. Latent stories overload even nearly empty places, as in "*Il Deserto Russo*". The connections of in-person encounters to film stills and street photography are almost inevitable, raising a perplexed question: do we become images of ourselves, or is it the other way around? Underlying the off-kilter familiar is Duehr's use of rhyming couplets throughout. While this could suggest a comfort of poetry-home, eccentric iambic-like pulses and unpredictable rhyme types are subtly unsettling. If the observed, in "Who Are You," seem "pitched headfirst into/This breathing world, without a single clue", the poem's title turns the view back around to us. We, it turns out, are other people's *Point Blank* enigmas.

David P. Miller,
author of *Bend in the Stair* and *Sprawled Asleep*

Point Blank

Gary Duehr

in case of emergency press
https://icoe.com.au
Travancore, Victoria
Australia

Published by in case of emergency press 2023

Copyright © Gary Duehr 2023
All rights reserved. Without limiting the rights under copyright reserved above, no part of this publication may be reproduced, stored in or introduced into a database and retrieval system or transmitted in any form or any means (electronic, mechanical, photocopying, recording or otherwise) without the prior written permission of both the owner of copyright and the above publishers.

ISBN: 978-0-6458496-0-8

Cover photograph: Gary Duehr
www.garyduehr.com

Acknowledgements

Some of these poems have appeared in *Apple Valley, Apricity Magazine, Bitchin' Kitsch, Cobalt Review, Conglomeration, The Courtship of Winds, Crack the Spine, Doubly Mad, Dual Coast, fir pin, Free State Review, Grey Sparrow Journal, The Moth, North of Oxford, Oddball Magazine, Pour Vida, Poydras Review, Literary Heist, Mudlark, Pangolin Review, Poesis, Poetry Pacific, Streetlight Magazine, Salamander, Smoky Blue Literary Magazine, Summerset Review, Transcendent Zero, Verdad, WINK,* and *Young Ravens Literary Review.*

Dedication

For Cammy Camille, who keeps it real

"WHAT IS SHE doing there?
A bag in hand, beside the road, a flare
Of sunlight on her face. Is there a bus
That's on its way, or has it dropped her off? Discuss."

from **Landscape with Heroine**

Table of Contents

One 1
    From the Future 3
    Arrivals 5
    Quick Vacation 6
    Terminal 7
    Super 9
    At LAX 11
    Déjà Vu Redux 12

Two 13
    Welcome to LA 15
    Sunset Strip 16
    In Living Color 17
    From Paradise 18
    Beachcomber 20
    Who Are You? 21
    City Of Angels 22

Three 23
    Il Deserto Russo 25
    What Degas Saw 26
    Geography 27
    Standard Oil 28
    Drive 29
    Landscape With Heroine 30
    Waiting For 31
    Odyssey 33
    White Sands 34
    Since Then 35
    The Sixties 36

Four 37
    Proof 39
    Beauty Myth 40
    Transition 41
    Geometry 42
    Zeroing In 43
    Woman In Phone Booth 44
    WALK / DON'T WALK 45
    Street Scene 46

Point Blank

Gary Duehr

One

From the Future

SO HERE THEY are, the passengers, striding toward us
With a sense of purpose—
From within a sterile vacuum
That's purposeless: a vast, white-walled tomb
Of aviation, like the one in LAX
In *Point Blank*, where Lee Marvin, in gray flannel slacks,
Is heading toward us with such menace.
His name? Walker, ironically. Discuss.
(Ah, those '60s terminals, their creamy gleam
Of sleek modernity, a fever dream
Of traveling into space.) In a year or so,
That group of strangers in the glow
Will be like us.
In fact, they'll *be* us, and us them. Thus:
They're coming from the future, that "great maw,"
According to Paul Strand, toward which the bourgeois
Rush headlong here and there.
And so we'll be condemned to that *nowhere*
Of layovers, delays, doomed to wander
DFW, LGA, some place we'd never
Go on holiday.
On the cover of *Non-Places* (Marc Augé),
An airplane's bulging nose
Is pressed against a lounge's plate glass, its pose
Just like a creature at a zoo.
And other views evoke this feeling too:
Strand's morning shot of Wall Street, circa 1915,
Of brokers late for work; or any scene

Of London, Paris, or Chicago.
A tiny detail lets you know
The city they were taken in. Here, there's none.
The walkway: blank, featureless, and everyone
A shadow in the distance.
It's like a vision of the afterlife, existence
As an endless, well-lit corridor.
And yet the basic question sticks: what's it all *for*?

Arrivals

DO RANDOM PEOPLE count
As separate categories? Is there a set amount
Of passengers who now arrive
In badly lit foyers—do they derive
Their looks from someone else?
They really might be other entities whose selves
Resemble someone famous.
Example A: that guy, his back to us,
Whose welcome kiss
Is for his wife or girlfriend. You can't dismiss
Coincidence in settings such as this:
His ragged haircut, his untucked shirt that fits
With what you can remember.
Location? Date? You have the picture
In your mind, nothing else, a few details.
And memory, such as it is, fails.
When did those clothes, that hairstyle
Come into being, then fade out? Has it been a while?
Of people, places, things, to prove that happenstance
We try to hold onto existence
Happened once to us. That's why
We need a photo ID at the gate, to pry
The past from who we are;
We're not that other person, we're not that TV star.
Is life that accidental, that much a fiction?
Yes and yes. That's why there's friction.

Quick Vacation

AND HERE'S A couple who's unhappy
Arguing in a crappy
Airport lounge. She's listening and she's not.
He's trying to explain, not out
Of urgency but as a way of killing time—
Which is already dead. Their crime?
The neurons in his brain are firing at their full capacity
While hers are barely flickering on, thanks to the rapacity
Of his interrogation.
Between them, an absence is evoked, a quick vacation
Of the senses. Colleagues, lovers, friends?
Maybe all of the above. It ends
With a whimper as she pushes back her hair
Behind one ear. There.
And on his lap is spread the daily paper
With a headline and a date, the way a kidnapper
Proves the victim isn't dead.
Beside them is a vacant chair, a shiny red
That's like an ad for emptiness.
In front of it a briefcase. No one's? Hers? Guess.
Like in a movie, it could contain a bomb
Or stacks of hundred dollar bills. Take your pick. Stay calm.

Terminal

AGAIN, WE WAIT. Again, we're stranded
At another airport, where we hunch, empty-handed,
On a bench, the six of us:
Pilot, co-pilot, and four flight attendants.
Boxy luggage at our feet.
How easy for us to accrete
Delays, frustrations, all the little tics
Of modern life no one can fix.
Waiting is our job: pure, unfiltered
Nothingness that stretches out ahead. The word
Itself, *wait*, just sits there too.
There's nothing to be done, nothing you can do:
Grab a coffee, browse the shops, hit
The restroom, make a call, or sit
And watch the human parade.
The six of us in uniform have made
Our final choice: no books, no drinks, no phones,
Nothing but exist. No one's
Alone and yet we all are,
As if we're stuck together in a stranded car.
Floor, bench, wall, that's it.
Nowhere to roam, no place to quit.
The wall and carpet bare, the light fluorescent.
Is there life beyond this moment?
Somewhere is there a complex narrative
That's been suspended, and we'll all start to live
Once *Play* is pushed? Cross, uncross
Our legs, that's all. Waiting is the sum of loss

Of everything that's ever come undone.
Think of Polish writer Ryszard Kapuscinski, he's the one
Who wrote of terminal ennui
At the airport in Yakutsk: how many
"Millions and millions… the world over pass the time
In such a passive way?" It's not a crime,
He said, to sit and stare,
Instead of torturing the counter clerk on where
The plane is now. There are no answers.
Think of all your sisters and brothers
In desert settlements, crushed by heat,
Or stuck in sleepy villages. He urged us to retreat
Into a deeper consciousness
That's not unlike a state of mental numbness.

Super

IT'S 1968.
There's a phone booth by the airport gate.
And in the phone booth there's a guy
Who's pushing hard against the glass, as if he's trying to fly
Like Superman. He can't.
He's stuck there, phone in hand; a boorish rant
Escapes his sideways grin:
"Just listen, pal, so what I'm sayin'... "
The glass cube of the phone booth offered Superman
What many came to understand
As little more than privacy's illusion.
For actual seclusion
A closet makes more sense. It's more the fact
Of being seen yet unseen in the act
That makes us a voyeur. Oblivious,
The salesman on the make ignores the obvious—
He's on display
Where everyone can see, the way
A monkey in a cage is.
In *The Human Zoo*, Desmond Morris writes our age is
Shaped by primal urges. That guy looks trapped
Inside the booth; his alter ego's apt
To smash the glass, not with a superpower
But just because he's superordinary—he's our
Exhibit A inside the vitrine
Like a formaldehyded shark by Hirst, Damien.
Behind him, in the shadowy recess
Of the airport lounge, a woman in a cocktail dress

Seems tuned in to his frequency
Like a scene from Wender's *Paris, Texas*, telepathically.
What if it's not an airport but the lobby of a bar
Or strip club, heavy with desire, where things can go too far?

At LAX

THERE IS A type of personality
Where ego has been lost. There's no normality.
The only reason to exist
Is as a product in the marketplace: to list
One's features, history, reviews.
No longer human, a thing to buy and use.
Consider now this business guy
At LAX who's looking bored, his eye
Has fixed upon a glass partition;
He's surprised to see he's standing there—this strange condition
Makes him grip his cellphone.
An inner dislocation? A sense that he's alone
Even in the chaos that is LAX?
Before he can relax
Up speaks his shadow self: "You think you're you?
You're not. It's not a pas de deux.
You think you're in control
Of what you say and do, but I am not your secret soul—
I'm you. That's right. We dress the same,
We act the same, we aim
To mitigate as best we can this psychic crisis:
Is what is *is*?
I'm not your fucking mirror, Jack,
I'm a thousand tiny data points that track
What's left of who you are.
Is that your face or mine? A scar
You recognize? Tell me, what's your view
On how you're different from a photograph of you?"

Déjà Vu Redux

AH, HERE WE are at last.
Where?, you ask.
In JFK's departure lounge. And every place
Is taken. I see your face
Shift from excitement into resignation.
You have to sit and wait, regardless of your destination.
It makes no difference
If you're traveling alone or not, your presence
Is all that matters now. Relax.
It's time to face the facts.
Outside the huge, curved window, the sky
Is fading into gray. Why?
It's just the way it is. And are we fading too?
Perhaps, like morning fog. There's nothing we can do.
On takeoff, each of us grows gray and pale,
More slight, more insubstantial,
Until we gradually dissolve into the ether.
It's like our will to persevere
Is slipping too, the urge to just *appear*.
Yet there's no fear.
No jokes, no kids, no walking wounded.
How could there be? No one's walking, no one's undead.
Garry Winograd once said that taking pictures
Is "the closest thing to not existing," which is
Similar to Walker Evans'
Theory of his own objective "non-appearance."
What if not existing means
That no one else does either? At JFK, the scene is
Like an endless limbo.
No one's going anywhere, though everyone must go.

Two

Welcome to LA

HERE'S SOME ON-STREET casting.
Three tough guys, huddled by the curb, like a lasting
Vision from some film clip:
A kid in shades, Marlboro at his lip,
Who's taking it all in.
The older dudes in Polo shirts, deep in conversation,
Intense as any Method actor.
From birth to death they'll stay in character,
In case a call to "Action!"
Booms out through the air—to catch one
Fraction of their life in celluloid
And so sidestep the void.
It's Miami or LA, somewhere too sunny.
The light is thin and bright, as crisp as money.
And the Oscar goes to… Best '80s Costume?
Best Weathered Face? Best Cigarette? To whom
Does this scenario belong?
Someone out of sight, beyond the throng
That's streaming down the street?
Anything could happen next. "A bite to eat?"
One of the Polo dudes could say. Or: "You're dead."
Maybe both at once: first lunch, and then a bullet to the head.

Sunset Strip

JUST LOOK AT all the stars
Embedded in the sidewalk: between the stares
Of prowling tourists, in the shiny glare
Of sun that's really setting. Where?
From way past Vine, beyond those figures lost in shadow.
A homeless guy, nowhere to go,
Is squatting on the edge
Of a wire-mesh trash bin, like it's a ledge
That he's about to jump from.
Wild-eyed, feral, he snarls at you: *I'm no bum.*
The light from stars, he rants, has died
Before it reaches you—a homicide or suicide?
I was born beneath the sign
Of Jack Daniels, no light was ever mine.
In fact, the garbage in this can is actually a diagram
Of my digestive system: who I am.
The stuff that goes through me goes through this whole city,
And it's not pretty.
You want respect, you voyeuristic motherfucker?
Then pay me what you owe me, sucker!
What's funny is, he looks a little bit
Like Paul Auster, the novelist, if Auster's work had turned to shit
Along with everything. And yet
The life that this guy leads, no debt
And no restraints, is not without attraction.
To blame the world, to bark at passersby—what satisfaction!
Nyargh, nngh, urghh, whatever.
I hear you, brother.

In Living Color

WALKING DOWN THE street in black and white
Like some vestige of the past—ghostly, slight—
Is not the same as walking down the street
In color. Particulars accrete:
Blond hair, red lips (a bit like Marilyn).
And in the distance a yellow sign
Against a clear blue sky.
It's cinematic, Technicolor. Why?
In color, everyone is walking toward the future,
Suddenly aware what's pure
And what's gone missing from the *mise en scene*:
What has been... then.
There isn't any grayish tint
Like fog on faces in the crowd, no metallic glint
Standing in for sky.
No, that big blue sky could magnify
The sense that something else exists
Beyond our everyday concerns, our checklists
What to do. We've been there,
Out in space, the vast expanse of air
That stretches overhead. In fact,
Every hour of every day, we're tracked
By satellites that spin and squawk
Around this bumpy rock.

From Paradise

IT LOOKS LIKE something has just happened
To this nice young couple—to what end
It's hard to tell.
Caught in traffic, arm in arm, well,
They don't look happy. In fact, they seem to cling
To one another: her hand is clutching
At his jacket sleeve, his fingers tensed into a fist.
But what, exactly, is it
That worries them? Have they just come
From bad news at a doctor's? Or has some
Other trauma hit them, like a separation?
In Milton's take on that explulsion
From Paradise, he writes, "Some… tears they dropped,
But wiped them soon." Something's stopped
This wife and husband in the middle of the crosswalk.
Maybe they just need to talk
And calm each other down. They're not remarkable,
This ordinary-looking couple,
And yet they catch the eye. According to Camus,
The present shows its residue
In every gesture.
So what is haunting in this picture?
What if it's looking forward
Forty years, out of the past tense, toward
A future tragedy that freezes passersby—
It shocks them, they can't cry—
In the aftermath of any modern city.
As Philip Roth once wrote of history,

It is "relentless, unforeseen."
It always lies in wait. It *can't* be seen.
As if the couple huddles close together
In anticipation of the news, for worse or better.

Beachcomber

WHICH ONE OF these
Isn't like the others? In the stale-beer breeze
In Venice Beach, it could be he's the one
Who has a Charlie Manson
Glazed look in his eye, his dirty hair
Swept back beneath his shades. His chest: bare.
His beard: a mess.
Any tourists idling by could guess
How tightly wound he is, a walking ad
For feeling bad,
For Multiple Anxiety Disorder.
Just like a Dylan song, south of the border,
In Juarez in the rain.
He's got that line stuck in his brain,
Around and round, a loop
That makes him feel he's trapped. But here's the scoop:
He might be fine, nothing wrong at all.
What makes his eyeballs crawl
Could be a sudden flash of ocean light
That strands him in this moment. It's *alright*,
You'd like to say to him, *this bad trip will not last.*
It too will pass, and like the past
Retreat into obscurity. What is the possibility
Another universe exists, completely different, a bright posterity?
Some place that's far way from here—
If only we could disappear.

Who Are You?

"WHO IS IT that can tell me
Who I am?" asks Lear. Or, conversely,
"You talking to me? You talking to me?"
Inquires De Niro of the mirror, as he
Whips out a gun.
It could be anyone
Who tells us with a sideways glance
Who we might be, a chance
Encounter on a busy city street
With boys and girls of summer in the heat:
A Mickey t-shirt, sun-streaked hair,
The casual indifference like they couldn't care.
But which of these
Will be the one to recognize, with ease,
Just who we really are?
There are so many faces in the world; it's bizarre
With so few basic options—
Eyes, mouth, nose, chin—that these conditions
Haven't led to duplicates
Filling up the planet. Zadie Smith, the essayist,
Describes the daily pleasure
Of watching "other people's faces" at her leisure.
To Garry Winogrand, photographer, it's all a game,
How many faces he can fit into the frame:
As if they're pitched headfirst into
This breathing world, without a single clue.

City Of Angels

SO WHAT REMAINS?
When all the major losses, plus the gains
Are tallied at the end,
When you're right where you still pretend
You really want to be—what then?
What is there to defend?
You find yourself, as many people do,
Adrift between one's dreams and what is true,
Just like the city of LA.
As if there were no other way.
But right now on the corner of the Boulevard,
Let's take an inventory: a shard
Of broken glass, some paper plates, a hot dog bun—detritus
By the curb that any one of us
Could stumble through. And nearby there's a shopping cart
Flipped on its back, a wounded animal, not from a supermarket
But from a life of desolation.
Or is it dereliction? When there's an abdication
Of one's will, when getting very sick
Or getting fired's the final kick
In the gut, and you no longer hold a place
In this world, you face
A shopping cart's reality that's crammed
With everything you own, as if to say: I am.
And when that cart goes belly up,
So do you, beyond the unimaginable, full stop.
A male hustler on the street—
Dyed blond curls, shades, short shorts—won't meet
The tourists' gaze, who carefully step around the mess.
Who among us will bear witness?

Three

Il Deserto Russo

HOW MUCH OF any modern city
Looks like a scene from some Italian movie:
A freeway's arc, the vast expanse
Of shimmering cement, and standing in the distance
A figure, solitary.
It's all so '70s. Yes, very.
And in a vacant lot—
Think money drop or Watergate's Deep Throat—you've got
More to do than parking cars.
It's just the kind of place where cameras
Are set up to surveil, the type of architecture
That's featureless, anonymous, and pure.
There's a sense of expectation.
When someone stumbles by, in anticipation
Of a crime—half-hidden by a wall—
They're about to take a fall.
Welcome to the world of double-crosses,
To a universe of pointless losses.
It's a world where people can get framed,
Literally, since everything is aimed
At geometric nothingness, except for doors and roof,
For beige and gray. A vacuum. A proof
Where narrative is poised to flow.
Enter: a car with tinted glass. Cue: some jazz, a solo
Saxophone, a muted bass.
Those flowers on the corner give a taste
Of oozing blood, a bullet wound
That blossoms suddenly, without a sound.

What Degas Saw

SO MUCH THESE days is accidental—
Odd, cut-off, ephemeral—
As any snapshot. Even with Degas,
In "Place de la Concorde," 1875, he saw
A fragment of the *Vicomte* as he
Was strolling with *His Daughters*—what was he
Thinking of, cigar in teeth? Their dog preoccupied
With something out of frame, as were they all, as if they eyed
An exit strategy.
And so they stood there in the open, anxiously.
According to MOMA's Curator Kirk Varnedoe, the harsh collisions
Of living in the modern world owe an allegiance
Not to photos but to paint.
One hundred fifty years ago, a general complaint
Crept in to taint our view.
He says that isolated strangers on the street are nothing new:
A jogger striding down the avenue
To make the light, a few
Business types and cyclists jostling past.
It's over in a second. Nothing lasts.

Geography

HOW IS IT possible, like one
Of Hopper's mournful women, to be on the run
And yet stuck at a gas pump
Or in some office dump?
How can they seem so existentially lost
When every leaf and doorknob is precise? As if the cost
Of loneliness
Is physical, emotional paralysis.
They look as if they're there
And not there—a kind of nowhere.
Or take this woman in a phone booth
On the phone. What is her truth?
Her mind is clearly elsewhere,
Connected to an abstract other through the air.
Or is that shadow actually not a phone?
Her chin rests on her hand, as though, alone,
She's thinking through her place.
There's no expression on her face.
She might as well be in a lobby, taking tickets
For a movie. *Only the Lonely?* Anyone? Anyone? (*Crickets.*)
She seems suspended there, as time is
Stretching out. Reflected in the glass and chrome which rhymes
The wrought-iron fence
With passersby in dark blue suits. There is a sense
This moment lasts for decades. Now take a closer took.
You see the title of the book
In her bag: "The Woman Who Rode Away"
By D. H. Lawrence. Is that her dream? To find her way
Into the vast high desert
Of New Mexico, a Georgia O'Keefe ascetic convert?

Standard Oil

THERE'S NOTHING HERE to see. Relax.
Beside a Coke machine, a guy who acts
As if he's in a movie
Puffs on a Marlboro Light. It's moody;
Nothing's happening except
For blue sky, gas pumps, asphalt. Here's the precept:
"Nothing comes from nothing" (*Lear*).
If there's no plot, no drama here,
Then what is there to witness
Other than the act of witnessing? Unless:
Like Ruscha's oil of LA's County Museum on fire,
His Standard Station goes up as well, higher
And higher the orangish flames, the pall of smoke—
A kind of art world in-joke.
(One thinks of Hopper's lonely station too
Along a Truro road, its bluish hue.)
So why would anybody stop and gaze?
Because of all the ways
That red and white can coexist:
Coke and t-shirt, billboard sign for Listerine, amidst
The crimson pumps, a pack
Of cigarettes, flattened on a tire track.
Near the end of one's career
The details tend, like Claude Monet's, to disappear.
And yet these vivid colors
Must have been here all along, a universe
Of nothingness before the Big Bang.
And little else to do but have a smoke and hang.

Drive

WHAT'S GOING ON? What's your obsession?
As always, that's the question.
Here's the scene: along a curving drive, some guys
In suits and ties and what could be their wives
Are getting in or out
Of cars. A funeral? Reception? Without
More info it's impossible to tell. This temporary lull
Is all so minimal.
Perhaps it's just a dream-like manifestation
Of our own hesitation,
As signaled by the balding guy
Who's scratching at his head as if he's wondering why.
What psycho-social weight
This gesture holds, an existential checkmate!
As if he wants to ask what we all ask:
What's really going on? Our task:
To calculate each triangulated elbow,
Each quarter turn of head, each flare of shadow
On cement. As if the key
Could be teased out photographically.
In fact, the more abundant
Evidence there is—closed circuit, dash cam—the more we want
To see another angle, fill the gap.
Why one white dress, the others black? Is it a trap
To zero in on how the sun
Is glancing off the branches of the evergreens? Is that a gun?
I'm reticent to make
Too much of this. So much these days is fake.
But what is happening here? How many lives
Are intersecting for a moment? Who lives, who dies?

Landscape With Heroine

WHAT IS SHE doing there?
A bag in hand, beside the road, a flare
Of sunlight on her face. Is there a bus
That's on its way, or has it dropped her off? Discuss.
Speeding by her, in a fraction of a second, we see
Her latent history:
Waiting, boarding, disembarking, a moment
Expanded in one's mind—just like the existential torment
Of a Hitchcock heroine.
Above her, the grayish clouds have broken
As a storm recedes; the rolling hills
Have been imprinted with their ragged frills.
The landscape is so vast,
So empty, like the American West, the last
Place for her to run.
She could be anyone.
And so could you as you drive by, addicted
To the need to find someone afflicted.
Now picture how the narrow road
In winter's swept with snow, an unforgiving cold.
You wish you could reverse
The flow of time, give her a ride, rehearse
The scene where you both realize
That time is running out, as you gaze in her eyes.

Waiting For

THESE TWO HOMBRES could be in a film, a scene
Where nothing happens, in between
What happens in the real story. What if the film's about
The actual *act* of waiting? The pangs of doubt
That come from sitting by a road
Beside a telephone pole? At night it could get cold.
To symbolize the human condition?
How we're all veering toward perdition?
In times like these, philosophy is worthless.
We're all just ordinary people, waiting to confess.
But if this *were* a film, their stark black suits,
Their luggage in the dirt, the barren fields, would be our cues
That things aren't going well.
We've seen this shot before, and we can tell
It's all been done: *Print!* Fini.
That mound of earth beside a hole looks funny.
Could it be an empty grave?
Who is dying? And who is there to save?
Has there been a tragic accident
And these the lone survivors? Or is it meant
As metaphor, a buried allusion?
Think Alabama, mid-'50s, post-Depression.
Not that this is any help to us.
Or them. Welcome to the U.S.
Of A. It's not as if they're at a bus stop.
No bus will ever come. No cop
Will cruise by anytime soon. They're on their own.
Perhaps they're on the lam, their cover blown.

For now, they guard their suitcases
By sitting on them, as shadows hide their faces.
But what if there's another possibility?
That they're musicians, out on tour; their immobility
Is temporary, waiting for a plot to set them into motion?
Here on this island in a windswept ocean.

Odyssey

SO WHAT WOULD happen if the monolith
In Kubrick's film, the one with
Apes and astronauts, landed on the street
In Cincinnati at the feet
Of people going to the office, on an ordinary day?
The answer: nothing much. It's just the way
That human beings are built.
We're all preoccupied. We think: will it
Make me late? It's like the story of a lump of shit
A guy finds in the middle of his plate. "I'll eat around it"
Is his ultimate conclusion.
So in response to this totemic intrusion,
What else is there to do? If something blots out
All of our attention, as Commander Dave drops out
Into a bedroom in Versailles
Beyond the infinite, it's pointless to ask why.
And yet, in Cincinnati, Ohio,
We wonder what that thing is. *Me oh my-oh.*
The back of a gigantic phone booth?
A sunlit slice of skyscraper? No matter what the truth,
The buses will still run,
The flags will flap above the Woolworth's, and everyone
Will weave along the sidewalk's crush.
That is, until an asteroid's big smush.

White Sands

AND HERE'S THE happy family
On vacation in the desert: brother, baby,
Mom and Dad, stranded in a patch
Of nothingness, just sand and sky. To catch
Some sun, have a noonday picnic?
They're heading straight for the horizon, a trick
Of distance their eyes play—
Who can tell how far away?
And why are they in such a hurry?
The Chevy door stands open, as if they worry
They might miss an eclipse
Or even, in this no-man's land, Apocalypse.
No shadow breaks the brightness anywhere.
No distinctive features marking here from there.
The four of them make for the line
Of sky, where there's a stretch of cloud, a spine
Of white on blue. A distant mountain?
There's a sense of something wrong, a tension
Between what's here and not.
Have they all just arrived? Is it their lot
To move and keep on moving, to leave
The safety of the car's interior to order to retrieve
What's just beyond the frame?
There's nowhere they can go, no aim.
No road in sight, which begs the query:
How did they get here? It's all very
Ambiguous, to say the least. The only thing that's true
Is car, sand, blinding swirl of blue.
Maybe what they're walking into is the future,
Where everyone is smiling in the picture.

Since Then

ACCORDING TO THE British poet Philip Larkin,
Fucking didn't begin
Until 1963. Just as a modern color photo
Didn't exist until a show
By William Eggleston at MOMA in the '70s.
And yet look at the cheese
That's bubbling on this pizza in a candid pic
From 1964. The color's so intense you want to lick
The cardboard box
Balanced on a car seat. The picture rocks:
A hunk of Ford, a fleshy hand, some 'za, a beer—
Yeah, it's all here.
And then there's something funny
In the corner; the photo's caught a monkey
Reaching for a Bud. As if the species has evolved
Into a love of beer and pizza. Resolved:
How radical this photo must have seemed
Back in the '60s. Few dreamed
That color could be everything. In black and white
That's on another roll, in bright daylight
The whole parade is rolling by: a beauty queen
With her tiara; the monkey can be seen
Behind her in the open car,
Its handler riding shotgun like the Secret Service. How far
We've come since then.
No motorcade may pass this way again.

The Sixties

LISTEN UP TO British novelist L. P. Hartley:
The past is like a foreign country.
Or is a foreign country
Like the past? Think England, circa 1960.
The air feels older. The clothes,
The color of the sky, the shadows
Stretched out from the trees—they all look soft.
As does this gravel path, the way the light falls off
Its crumbling edge. As if a photograph
Has muted over time. Don't laugh.
This family could be mine.
Or yours, ambling in the park. How they're all trying
To have some fun: a bike, a tennis racket,
A sunny afternoon. They're backlit
As the five of them (Mum and Dad, the kids) approach the lens,
Half-smiling, in a line. You sense
That nothing could go wrong inside this scene.
Jump forward 50 years. What does it mean
When everything around you shifts? When every open field
Could be a target for a drone, its deadly yield?
Imagine now a brilliant flash
That fixes each of them, like Pompeii effigies, in ash.

Four

Proof

PEOPLE LEAD THEIR lives. Things happen.
No matter where or when,
The usual takes place or not:
The ups and downs, the push and pull. You take your shot
And hope that things work out.
They either do or don't. You can't walk out,
You have to go the distance.
First growing up, then puzzling your existence,
The cosmos questions you, then *poof*.
Here's a sample proof:
Imagine there's a cast of characters
Who populate a film; we watch them make their errors
Over time, the way we scan
The swarming sidewalks of Manhattan
For any familiar faces.
Consider these young women, the subtle ways
They clutch their hands: a purse,
A wrist, a strand of hair, a ring. What's worse?
The fact that they each reoccur
A decade later, played by different actors, or your
Obsession with their mystery?
There is another history
In which these hands are seen.
In Rembrandt's *Night Watch*, amidst the sheen
Of silk and lace, they clasp a gun
Or point offstage or beat a battle drum. Everyone
Is headed toward their fate
Along the crowded New York streets. Just wait.

Beauty Myth

YOU SEE HER. You try not to stare.
On the sidewalk, underneath a poof of platinum hair
A woman holds a tissue
To her nose. Her left eye's black and blue.
She's hurt. A swollen patch of gauze
Obscures her other eye. The cause
Is hard to tell.
A face lift that's gone wrong? A private hell
Exploded into public? In her chic mesh shift
She looks bereft, as if
She's in a Francis Bacon portrait, raw and flecked
With blood. You feel for her, this wounded object.
The bracelet on her wrist looks like an ID
From a hospital. It might be.
And on it, does it say, "Do Not Resuscitate"?
Your presence gives you guilt—the weight
Of circumstance is too much.
The social critic T. Adorno claims the female character, as such,
When glamorized, humiliates all those who witness it.
Her dress is not a dress, it
Becomes a bandage too, one that tries
To cover all our eyes.

Transition

THERE ARE THINGS you need to lug
From place to place: a grocery bag or amp you hug
Against your chest
To climb the stairs, plus all the rest
You drag along the street. The side effect?
When everything's dropped off, the boxes checked,
You feel a little freer: behind a cigarette,
Above a cup, there's no regret.
Hey, look at those two guys
Who pull a rack of clothes, the brilliant dyes
Of scarlet, orange a flame
Against the street's expanse. They aim
Across the busy intersection.
Even Sisyphus with his heavy load would now and then
Take a lunch break.
Is that the plan? Or are these coats and jackets fake,
Costumes for a Broadway spectacle?
Perhaps the show is *this*, a Midtown full
Of taxis, trash bags, grit and grime, the passersby
An ever-changing cast who try
To shoulder through the throng, their bulky encumbrances
Like second selves or extra appendages.

Geometry

SO WHAT IS black and white
Walking down the street? That's right—
Two nuns in their habits. It's all geometry:
Between their arms, a V
Is echoed by the angle of the crutches
Of the woman with a bandaged foot, which is
Balanced on its heel.
The whole thing seems unreal.
Is there a hidden story here or not?
Perhaps a parody, somewhat, of *Some Like It Hot*.
There is a folded note
Clutched in the taller sister's hand; behind her, in a winter coat,
A man is sneezing in a Kleenex,
As if her piece of paper, through cinematic special effects,
Has blown up in his face. What does this scene
With all its chaos, mean?
Where is the focus, the protagonist?
And which are minor players who exist
For local color or to lend an ear?
Nothing's clear.
Let's put the blame on the photographer, whose burden
Is to see obsessively, even when uncertain
What the outcome is.
For instance, this random street shot like a pop quiz.

Zeroing In

I'VE SEEN THAT face, that's *her*,
Staring straight out from a picture
At whoever's watching. Or maybe she comes later,
In photos not yet snapped. She's so familiar.
Around her, in Midtown, the flux and flow
Of people on the go. You know:
Briefcases, bags in hand—behind their sunglasses
A frown of anxiousness. Everyone passes
Without a second look.
Some teens, a woman with a hardcover book
Clutched to her chest, and in a straw hat
A guy who points dramatically, as if he's at
A carnival. In the crush
She stands alone, unaffected by the rush.
Blond hair, dark eyes, in white, a Hitchcock heroine
From some film, someone we zero in on
In a crowd—who gazes back at us
A little nervously. Should she jump on that bus?
What's next for her? The future
Closes in on her. It's a trap, this picture.
So what's the lesson? That fate
Can freeze us in our tracks, and while we wait
To grab a second chance, there's been
A switch, a con. A screen
Clouds up our vision. It's all about deception.
Are we then guilty by association? Or the one exception?

Woman In Phone Booth

IN THE INTERVAL between
What's glimpsed and what's unseen,
Between the hidden and the big reveal,
There's a kind of ballet. You feel
That everyone's complicit:
The passersby, the looker and the looked-at, who each elicit
A grin or frown of disapproval.
And at the center of it all
A woman in a phone booth
Like Houdini's water torture. What's her truth:
Her face is half-obscured
In shadow; the phone receiver's covered
By her right hand. Maybe she's about to say,
Some guy is taking pictures. There's something in the way
She faces us. Does she feel our hesitation?
Her eyes are lowered in discretion
At this private tête-à-tête
That's playing out in public. And yet
Isn't this a conversation
With all the other photographs whose *raison*
Prefers to be anonymous?
What does that say about us?

WALK / DON'T WALK

POISED THERE AT the curb, waiting for the light
To switch to WALK, it's fight
Or flight, like suspects in a line-up. Fact:
There's something in the act
Of queueing that brings out aggression.
Just look at them, their faces pinched, standing at attention.
One guy is grasping something in his hand—
A crumpled sack or rock. Please understand
How quickly things devolve
As masks fall off, and what's considered norms dissolve.
The tall kid who's slumped down is me
In high school. Gee.
My father shouted, "Stand up straight,
Your shoulders back, chest out. Accept your fate."
I have, I have. Look the world back in the eye
No matter what. Remember how high
Giacommeti's sculptures loom, all bone and skin:
Exclamation points stretched thin.

Street Scene

SO HAVE YOU heard the one
About the older woman and the nun?
One afternoon they meet
On the sidewalk of a busy street.
The nun is bending down
To help the woman, who's fallen to the ground.
Her bloodied head is resting on a shopping bag.
All time has stopped; there's a lag
While bystanders stand by:
A student, a young girl, some office workers; every eye
Is focused on the accident.
They're so composed, so still; it's like an incident
From a foreign movie by Renais
Or Antonioni—the way
A tragedy, out of nowhere, can interrupt
An ordinary day. It's that abrupt.
And have we seen this cast before?
A victim, a nun or cop, the ballet corps
Of passersby who blend
Into the scene and stop to see what happened?
Consider how the writer Roberto Calasso
Describes the many lives and deaths amidst the flow
Of myth, and yet a novel's character
Gets a single gesture.
As do we. See how the injured woman's white glove
Is curled up on her chest, as the nun looks on above.

About the Author

Based in Boston, Gary Duehr teaches writing and photography at local universities. His MFA is from the University of Iowa Writers Workshop. In 2001 he received an NEA Poetry Fellowship, and he has also received grants and fellowships from the Massachusetts Cultural Council, the LEF Foundation, and the Rockefeller Foundation. His books include *America Hurrah, SORRY, In Passing, Potato Chips for Dinner, Beautiful Bullets, Winter Light,* and *Where Everyone Is Going To.*

www.garyduehr.com

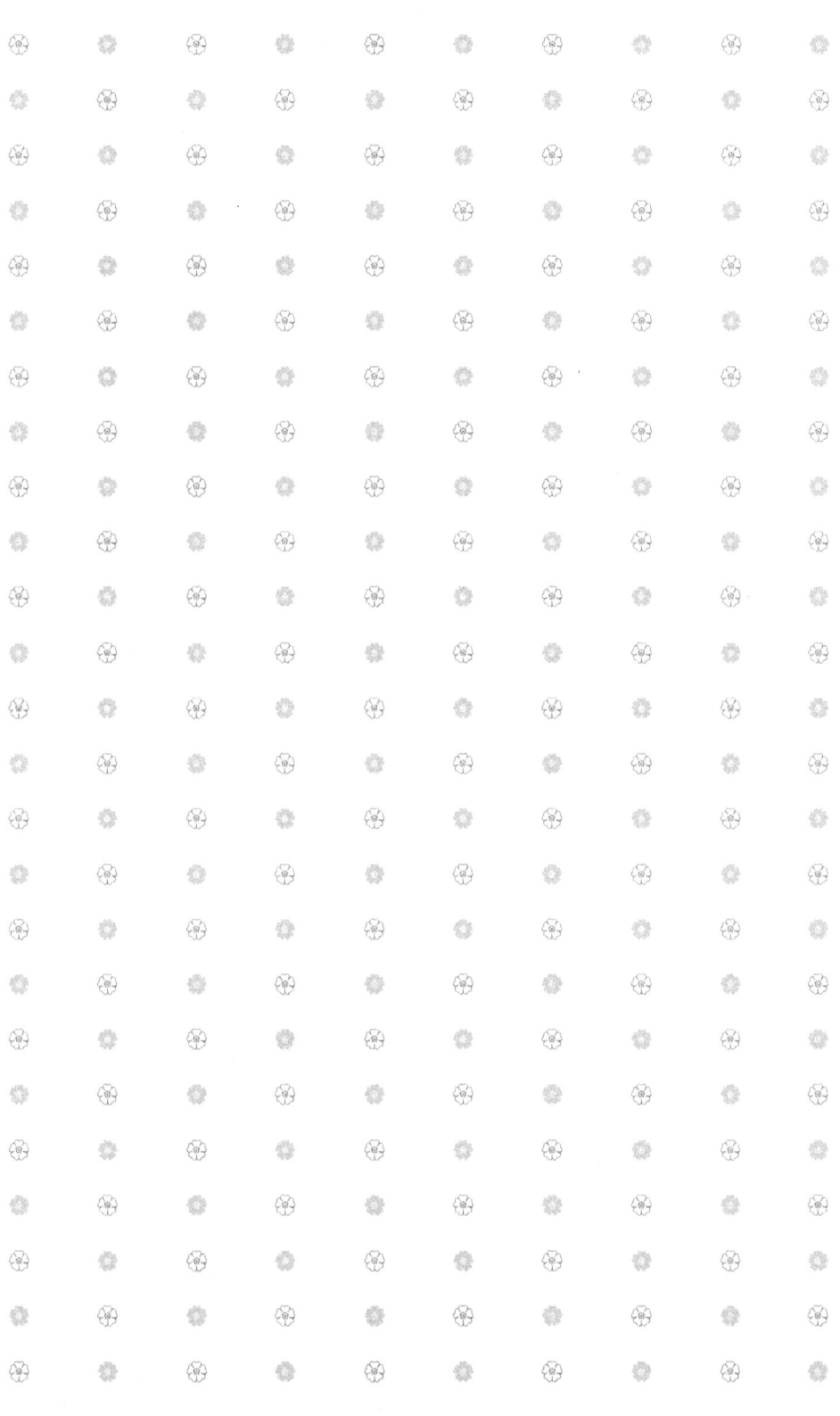

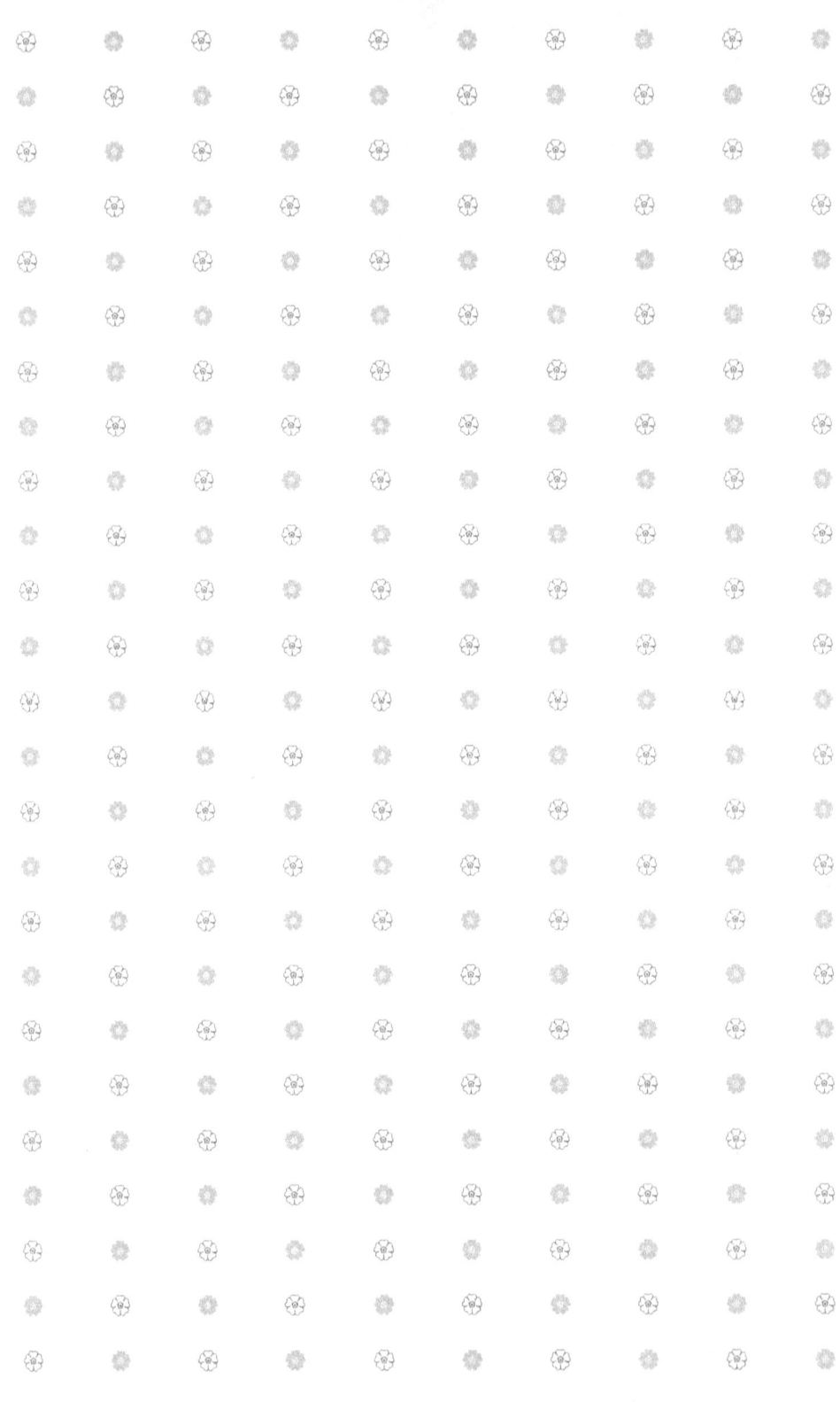

www.ingramcontent.com/pod-product-compliance
Lightning Source LLC
Chambersburg PA
CBHW030303010526
44107CB00053B/1801